CARL PHILLIPS

The Tether

CARL PHILLIPS is the author of four books of poems, including *Pastoral* and *From the Devotions*, a finalist for the National Book Award. He is the recipient of a 2001 Academy of Arts and Letters Award in Literature and of fellowships from the Guggenheim Foundation and the Library of Congress. He is professor of English at Washington University in St. Louis.

THE TETHER

THE TETHER

CARL PHILLIPS

Farrar, Straus and Giroux

New York

Farrar, Straus and Giroux
18 West 18th Street, New York, NY 10011

Copyright © 2001 by Carl Phillips

Printed in the United States of America
Published by Farrar, Straus and Giroux in 2001
First paperback edition, 2002

Library of Congress Cataloging-in-Publication Data
Phillips, Carl, 1959–
  The tether / Carl Phillips.— 1st ed.
    p. cm.
  ISBN: 978-0-374-52845-4
  I. Title.

PS3566.H476 T4 2001
811'.54—dc21

                              00-045611

Designed by Lynn Buckley

www.fsgbooks.com

P1

For Doug—

CONTENTS

August–December

January–May

something that maybe I   could bargain with
and make a separate peace   beneath
within   if never with.

Elizabeth Bishop

AUGUST–DECEMBER

LUCK

What we shall not perhaps get over, we
do get past, until—innocent,
with art for once

not in mind, *How did I get here,*
we ask one day, our gaze
relinquishing one space for the next

in which, not far from where
in the uncut grass we're sitting
four men arc the unsaid

between them with the thrown
shoes of horses, luck briefly as a thing
of heft made to shape through

air a path invisible, but there . . .
Because we are flesh, because
who doesn't, some way, require touch,

it is the unsubstantial—that which can
neither know touch nor be known
by it—that most bewilders,

even if the four men at
play, if asked, presumably,
would not say so, any more

than would the fifth man, busy
mowing the field's far
edge, behind me,

his slow, relentless pace promising
long hours before the sorrow
of seeing him go and,

later still, the sorrow
going, until eventually the difficulty
only is this: there was some.

JUST SOUTH OF THE KINGDOM

It is for, you see, eventually the deer to
take it, the fruit

hangs there. Meanwhile, they
graze with the kind

of idleness that suggests
both can be true: to see—and seem

not to—the possible danger of
us watching;

to notice, and to also
be indifferent to the certain

plunder of, between them
and us, the lone

tree, thick with apples the deer have
only to nose

up against,
what's ripe will fall, will

become theirs.
—A breeze, slightly—

in which, if nobody, nothing moves,
nevertheless when it comes to

waiting it is useless,
understand, to think the deer

won't outlast us. They have,
as do all animals before the getting

tamed, a patience that
comes from the expectation of,

routinely, some hungering.
Ourselves, we are bored easily:

how much time can
be left before—as toward, say,

an impossible suitor whom already
we've kept long enough

baying—we'll turn away, and
begin the life I've heard tell of?

The light is less, there. One of us
has betrayed the other.

SPOILS, DIVIDING

Thank you for asking—
yes,
I have thought on the soul,

I have decided
it should not be faulted for
its indifference: that is as it

must be.
How blame
the lantern whose limits

always are only the light of
itself, casting the light
out?

That the body enjoys
some moment
in that light, I regard

as privilege.
                Say what
you will.

The hawk's shadow
darkening
the zeroed-in-upon prey,

the victim
classically becoming
quite still—

        It is very
like that. Having
understood which, I admit to

—also—the body as mere
story
whose ending,

like the story itself, is
small—how
not to think, for a time, that it

is not finished,
                        though it
is finished—

The ending was always this one.
Prediction,
gift,

science.
What shines now doesn't, won't
in our lifetime

stop shining—
                no.
I turned away.

WORDS OF LOVE

Don't.
When I point
out to you that

the flat face of the lake's water in
stillness is made suddenly
more striking for how a wind

just now, coming, spoils it,
I have in mind
only how even a least

disturbance, strangely
heightening a thing's
beauty, can at last

define it. *Don't*
go, I mean,
possibly. If I have

described us
as a reasonable but flawed kind
of proof of

some fact that I keep
forgetting, I might have
added that not

only do I respect, I
require mystery.
Less and less

am I one of those who believes
To know a thing,
first you touch it

—as among the blind, or
as among such as are
more inclined than

ourselves, lately, to living on
life's reportedly still perilous, still
exhilarating

edge. Ourselves
exhausted,
even as a child's body, sometimes, will

fall toward sleep out of sheer
waiting,
uncertainty,

how will the story end?
There was, one time, a stag . . .
And now there isn't,

is there?
And no, he won't come,
ever, back. This is the widening, but

not unbeautiful wake of his having
left us, and this
is the light—

true,
exotic,
faded slightly—in which

much, still, is possible:
Don't promise—
Don't forget—

THE POINT OF THE LAMBS

"The good lambs
in the yellow barn—the rest
housed in blue." By

"the rest," meaning those who
—the guide explained—inevitably
arrive suffering. "For

some do," he added.
Soft.
Serious. This—like

a new lesson. As to
some among us, it was,
it seemed. The usual

stammer of heart the naïve
tend to, in the face of what finally
is only the world. What

must it be, to pass
thus—clean, stripped—
through a life? What

reluctance the mind
shows on recognizing
that what it approaches

is, at last, the answer
to the very question it knows
now, but

too late,
oh better to never to have never
put forward. What I

mean is we moved
closer,
in,

to the blue barn's
advertisement—
flaw,

weakness. We
looked in.
Three days, four days

old. Few expected to
finish the evening it was beginning to
be already. And the small

crowd of us
shifting forward, and—
in our shifting uniformly—it

being possible to see how between
us and any
field rendered by a sudden wind

single gesture—kowtow,
upheaval—there was
little difference. Some

took photographs; most
did a stranger thing: touched
briefly, without

distinction, whichever
person stood immediately in
front of, next to. Less

for support than
as remedy or proof or
maybe—given the lambs who

besides dying, were as well
filthy (disease,
waste and, negotiating

the dwindling contract
between the two,
the flies everywhere)—

[15]

maybe the touching
concerned curbing the hand's instinct
to follow the eye, to

confirm vision. Who can
say? I was there—yes—but
I myself touched no one.

A FORCE, AND WOULD CONSUME US

Because the lawn is not ours, I can
mind less
its destruction—

the pale grubs that become daily
more legion; and, tearing
at them,

the shimmering consequence of crows,
stiff chorus, each cast in the special
black

of bad news—only, always, *what
is it?* Until that, too, not
mattering: winter soon,

and you—
and I—
We'll have left here,

changed presumably, to guess
from the steady
coming of us both to wanting, differently,

the body. Still, I want it
with you, steadfastness remains
one of my two gifts, the other

less gift, perhaps, than simply a matter
of *I can't help it*,
namely a knack for making anything

mean something.
You will have seen what
that leads to. Last night,

it was the train shedding town the way
every night it does, but
also, this time, like

answer: how easily can grow
routine even the chance any
train equals—*Now*

go   Now return   How could I
not wake you?
For reasons possibly not yours,

I want the sunset that
you want.
Of heroes,

what I most remember is
that gesture—in
defeat, victory, the same—that

each comes to:
regards, as if for the first time, his own hands.
Mutters, or is silent.

Translations are various: *God,*
If not for, If only—
Look what   I've done.

ROMAN GLASS

Even in the latter, raveling days of the republic, the Romans
    clung archaically, naïvely
to a belief in equal rule: each year, two consuls were still
    elected to govern—each
equally helpless, inconsequential.

If for nothing else, it's for at least his effectiveness and
    unwavering sense of priority
that Julius Caesar deserves our attention. As example:
    recognizing the folly of equal rule,
he quite efficiently—because literally—saw to the removal of
    his colleague and enemy

Pompey's head. Never mind that he is said not to have given
    such an order, that in public
he displayed revulsion upon being presented the head by his
    victorious army; Caesar is
sure to have admired in the soldiers, if not their loyalty—which
    virtue too, like

beauty, he understood as inherently flawed and therefore
    subject to erosion—then their
precision, their thoroughness, their refusal to compromise any
    more than had the blade
in the executioner's hand. Of course,

Caesar eventually was also murdered—but he prefigures and
    serves as immediate catalyst
for empire, a system which, though bloodier, was nevertheless
    more durable, hypnotic,
and worthy of study, hence the abrupt rise in the number of
    those wanting to chronicle

their own times. Granted, the poetry produced in this period
    remains (with a few
assumable exceptions) negligible in quality; but the prose
    flourishes, especially that which
gets written under the most brutal, and often violent laws of
    censorship. It is as

if restraint (often enough, a naggingly realistic fear for one's
    life) exerted upon prose—
and relentlessly—whatever pressure it is that, in effect, can
    render a poetry *from* prose,
in the way, say, sharded glass becomes other and newly valued,
    given a long enough

exposure to the ocean's necessarily indifferent handling. That
    piece in your hands now
—I found it just south of Rome, not far from the waters that,
    despite pollution, when
they receive the light reflected off the salmon-, sky-,
    oxblood-colored villas that front

the boat-littered bay of Naples, suggest something, still, of a
    grand history that is
finally holy, there being always a holiness attached to that
    which is absolute—even
should the subject prove, the entire time, to have been loss.

THIS, THE PATTERN

Of course, of course,
the doomed crickets. The usual—as if
just let go on their own
recognizance—few birds acting
natural, looking guilty.
Gray   black   gray.
You were right, regarding

innocence. A small pair of
smaller moths rising
parallel, simultaneous, ascent
itself the seeming axis for
what rotation? sex? combat?
joy as ritual and not quite green, more
yellow? Certain

other exultations.
You were right
the entire time. The end
of desire exactly where you
thought, once, you'd found it.
Blue, like you thought, the light
around him, the light

inside of which he sings
I lost my keys, my first compass,
a watch in the grass, sight of,
I lost my way.

Singing, as if no one had ever
before lost anything. He should
know better, the way

you do. In time
the field shifting utterly
until everything
far, everything remembered
is remembered dimly. Even
now something, for example, about
a fig tree—   And then,

it is useless, gone, the unrequired
evidence all over that you are never,
never wrong. So—
why weeping?
why mercy?
Already here comes
again the glittering accident of

you, stumbling free of—across—
the others.
A few scratches, mostly. And
gratitude, yes,
but gratitude this time as only the first
part. Soon enough: *What has happened,
it could happen again.*

STAGGER

As when the flesh is shown
to be remarkable
most, for once, because

markless:
where the bruise
was, that we called

a bell, maybe, or
—tipped,
stemless—

a wineglass, or just
the wine spilling
out,

or a lesser lake viewed
from a great height
of air,

instead the surprise that
is blunder when it
has lifted, leaving

the skin to resemble
something like clear
tundra neither foot nor

wing finds,
—or shadow of.
When did the yard get

this swollen—
mint, apples,
like proof of all that

anyway went
on, in our distraction?
When did the room

itself start
stirring with—distant, but
decidedly—the scent of

pines wintering, further
still, a not-very-far
sea—

MEDALLION

He must be calling from somewhere
very near
the water, I can hear it

behind what
he is telling me of
last night's

dream, which was sexual,
which was
unusual for its details.

It must be bright there
still. Afternoon-ish,
letting go.

Here, the wooded yard
blackens, becomes again
a new country, unstrung as

yet of streetlight.
No streets yet.
Because entering its dark feels

more like only
entering now,
further,

my life, it is less unsettling than
the first time.
I can, almost,

want the hearing and
not knowing which
one—human, animal—

moves, toward me,
the not having
to assign noise a name

more specific than *Some
mouths hungry,
Something tears at the late leaves.*

There must be, everywhere,
the water,
getting perhaps

unavoidably reduced to
blue
tumbling context, him

adapting quickly
to native custom, he
must resemble them

already, taking for granted
that which can hardly be
blamed for its own

abundance—it must
start, that way:
none of us meaning, anyone, any harm.

REGALIA FIGURE

We were mistaken, I think.

I think the soul wants
no mate
except body, what it has

already, I think
the body is not
a cage,

no,

but the necessary foil
against which the soul
proves it was always

true, what they said: to stand
unsuffering
in the presence of another's
agony is its own
perhaps difficult but
irrefutable pleasure.

That I might not have
thought so, without
you, I understand now.

Likewise, about the body
wanting most
only another body, the flesh
from within
lit as if with an instinct for,

endlessly, more
of itself, for
a joint suffering which,

if it too is a kind of pleasure,

if also the only one the body is
likely in this lifetime to

come into, how refuse?

Possibly—probably—there
was not ever a choice
anyway.

The revised version of
effortless.

The twice-plowed-
back-into-itself
field, the light
upon it,

the animal lives
inside the field, inside the light—

I am learning to pity
less what
lacks will entirely.

There are things worse than being
like that. —And yet,
to let go of it, ambition,
seems as impossible, as
impossible—

How extend forgiveness
insincerely? Meeting you,

I knew you utterly.
I saw, utterly,

this life.
I'd put it on.
I'd wear it like

—a crown, for
how it flashes.

STRUNG ABSENTIA

What happened

was less the fault of, more
the fact of
a nostalgia, to say

I missed things is
it precisely, the all but
unbearably lit
cropscapes—blue-&-soy,
splay, I-mean-to; visible from

miles, the weathered
verticals, like
anomaly on stilts and

corsaged, to say the thin
blades milling, making
more fine a wind
who has seen? I missed

what I'd grown into
admiring, the sight of a good man

astride a swift but
wasting horse, its eyes
attesting to hard days of,

equally hard, being ridden,

the rider himself aflush
already with the hero's
tendency toward
forgetting the exact number

of leagues crossed, of
lives that, inevitably,
in the crossing, must break.

What happened,
except history? Horses first;

and then trains,

and then the trains themselves,
if not yet quite history, at
least historical, it
seemed natural, easy

therefore, to give them
names like Chivalry,
Steadfastness . . . the one
by night I called
Innocence, despite knowing

it traveled no silver rail—
the rails, like the wheels, like
the couplings, not
rust, not bronze, some

other color, deeper than
familiarity, but
this side, still, of obliteration—

abrasion, maybe. Every night
the train, its music, figuring,

Like innocence, I kept
insisting until—
I didn't,

I became tired, as
who doesn't, having always

the truth, and not saying:

the train was never
innocence, that music at
most only something
like innocence, like the memory

of it—which,
oh, if noisier now than even
I'd expected, what has happened

but again, predictably,
misjudgment? I have been
wrong twice before—once
in the presence of a man

who'd begun of a sudden to
cry openly: I
believed it

best, I should let him;
softly, then—softly, I moved away.

RECUMBENT

Here, the ribs end, they—divide, into
double fans. Splay. And fall. I believe
the pictures—there

must be, therefore, the heart
underneath and off-centered, little
downbeat,

then not. The hair: important,
but the eyes more so, and the mouth, even
more. Every darkness. The limbs,

all along, obvious—arms, legs—
four workable unriddlings I ought not
to have had to come to by

guessing—for so long. The brain tonight
like a cavernful of small, constant
winds in front of which the ten

answers to the question *what mattered
most and, so, defined me?* disband,
assemble, in no order, any order:

ambition;
an instinct for correct color;
sex—as I want it and, after, as I can give it;

music, by which I mean as much water as I do the notes as I
    do the leaves;
fraternity—of love, the one shape I've found not difficult to
    find always;
words, but only when ordered as—as a rule—they have not
    been;

less the truth, than a way to frame it;
those losses which no inadequate guilt attends;
a devotion across which, let a bit of the flaw show;

human, reasonable,
the flaws . . .
Why regret?

Finally, nothing was
not marvelous. I remember the tongs. Clamps. Lighted coals;
other disappointments. I

remember the art of interposing
a distance between pain and
self—*where did that go?* some part of

the brain stirs at,
the mouth holds,
the breath carries,

the cock at ease already
inside that angle I call
blunted-arrow-how-now-make-your-mark

echoes,
the backside—once
stunningly broken phalanx, now broken

merely—also echoes. . . .
The knobs, the buttons. Iliadic,
vulnerable, the nipple. Cell

after cell, sort-of-labyrinth,
honeycomb, all the thick-with-its-own-sweetness
liquid walled in by pattern, by

regimentation until it isn't, until the walls fail,
neglected, the flesh a hive but
all the bees, classically,

smoked out.
I trusted the smoke, believed in the fire it must
mean, somewhere,

I remember the bellows—a kind of
heaven, the two hands, laboring
at them.

LUSTRUM

Not less; only—different. Not
everything should be visible.
Wingdom:

doves. Not everything
can be. There are many parts
to the body. *The light, like*

I said. Gratia exempli, per
person more than one
heart. As, of hearts,

more than one kind.
As coin.
As thrust. To begin

counting is to understand
what it can mean, to
lose track. Is there nothing

not useful? Anything
left, anymore, private? *Ambition,*
like they said: little torch;

having meant to. Doom is
always in style somewhere
and, where it isn't, will

come back. *Bird
in the bush, take me.* Splendor:
nothing priceless. To believe

anything, to want anything—these,
too, have cost you. *Flame,
and the beveled sword, set*

inside it. This one,
this—what did you think
body was? What did you

mean when you said
not everything should
be said? *The light as a tipped*

cone, searching. The body
that breaks
finally, routinely faltering

before that. *If a sword,
then without patience; if as
water—pearled, swift.* What else

could you have thought,
when you thought
love—having known

the torch, having more than
meant to. *Just watch me.* Not
grand; only—distant. *Weather,*

and the bleachable skull,
set inside it. Locust-wind, small
through-the-yellow-sycamore

fingering wind,
Carry me,
let the prayer—valiant, up—

go. Some bright and
last thing
should.

JANUARY-MAY

FOR THE FALCONER

The hunt—was good; the kill,

less so, as you'd said to
expect. I don't listen, always—

Plus the noise. Plus distraction:

the dogs, naturally, the boys
whose job it is to hem and then

beat at the brush, driving
the animal in, closer, toward
the men, the men beautifully

negotiating their mounts
meanwhile. Which part

don't you understand? Also

arrowheads, here a rainwashed
and single bone, relics everywhere
chipped and for the naming:

I love and *I mean to* and

—others. You'd said patience,
you'd said vigilance—*Watch,*

something will break through.

And indeed: first a pheasant,
then a fox, then a smallish

deer—each one of which no
sooner had stepped, panicking,
from cover,

the men would
bring, as they say, the game down. . . .

But none of these

what I'd wanted,
or want now.

I am not patient, as I'd
said to expect. You don't
listen, always—   Plus the horns,

plus the banners: of blue,

for diminishment, pale

resurrection yellow, already

the moon like a slightly
uptilted boat tugging
doggedly its soon-to-be-dark

cargo. And meanwhile, plenty
of light, still—

each could still see the other;
it would be entire;
and all at once—

Which part had you hoped
to hear: the boys at last done

with beating? the dogs leashed,
done retrieving? the men,

but now more distantly giving shout?

The field is yours, that
I stagger back to.

(come)

(what it most sounded like)

(plunder)

TETHER

I.

Small release—

Bird, risen, flown—

I woke,
all but weightless.

Himself, the weight—exactly—of eclipse.

II.

If the tree looked like insisting upon falling,

I'd let it fall.

Should you use force, and the forcing
give your skin a red cast as of light to
a night sky,
by which to know there
lies, somewhere,
a towndom,

I'll find the town; enter.

A piece of the wall,
a tower,
refused for a time
fire, and then burned?

> *Raise a glass. Grave a stone to it.*

III.

Darkest room—

from lightlessness
how slow, homing back—

what required?

> *when expect to?*

As across a distance, like the one between
this space

and that of God,
no measuring

touches,

quite,

except it fail—

⟋

Now he is standing over me

And now I have laid my body on his own

PREAMBLE

Almost, the body as
half-remembered, before trespass,
had left memory—

was there ever the sound
trains make? was there,
pausing,

an owl, too?
A belief in prayer
was no longer the same as believing

prayer could make what did not happen
from what happened. Just then,
the light fell

like compromise, like
the passing up of gold for
instead silver

upon the basil that,
let go,
had gone to flower: small, white, and

—stitch-like—
the cabbage moths tilting
misnomered

into, settling
on. It was all
but accomplished,

the seasonal arcing toward failure.
How long, again,
would be winter—

the trees leafless as
spent soldiers
who, whether they could or couldn't

imagine spring, in time
would rally: each
hoisting—green, temporal—his shield—

CHAMBER MUSIC

Like something broken of wing,
lying there.
Other than breathing's *rise, catch,*

release,
a silence, as of some especially wounded
animal that, nevertheless, still

is conscious,
you can see
straight through the open

eye to where instinct falters because
for once it has come
divided: to cry out

could bring rescue; would
mean announcing, as well,
weakness, the very

helplessness for which
hasn't all this time every gaped mouth been
but waiting?

I dislike weakness, I
sang to him,
him taking my good arm

like a kind of oar,
and him drowning,
and the water as wide as Bible

says,
and no dove—as if not
anywhere now a brightness to

that room:
only the brawl of the wind
making its here-and-there bits of

difference—to the curtain,
to a shirt
swelling like, inside it, a living body or

a boy's hair, for a time, lifting.
World of *nothing-to-*
constrain-me. Turn it over. Now do it again.

LITTLE DANCE OUTSIDE THE RUINS
OF UNREASON

Nothing about that life
was incidental:

the night's routine of
the night leaves, by the moon, being
shadow-cast against the white sides of the small but

there

garage, say;

the heart—
that it kept beating—

Nothing was ever itself
only, or allowed to be:
if a field,

then a field

of massacre, from which the bodies
have but recently been
lifted, the trampled

grasses just
beginning their spring, back,

the drowse of the kill, after,

and the difficult-to-
admit-to disappointment
at the loss of them, carnage's
bright details,

for what they meant of
vulnerability,
that softness which has seemed the body's
greatest truth . . .

To look at you,
looking that way—at me—

How scarified it is,
devotion's face—as from the labor of
too long accepting

substitution

over what it fears has been
nothing at all, certain

moments, of weakness.

Weakness, I think,
defined us most. We all but made of it

a country—

Let it fall.

Take my hand.

(Singing)
nothing unforgivable

(Singing)
everything to forgive

THE LOST CHORUS

One saying

We faltered, we
loved, oh—

we sailed—

the wondering
only is which,

and which one of us first

One saying

Because I
could not

Because I could

Because

(Rain somewhere, and the snow—
fitful, here.)

One saying

There's the bell again,
sounding like nothing remotely

like silver

Another
One of us should answer it

Another
Who?

One by
one by

more

(who have always been everywhere
about us,

we had only to notice)

do they
come to us,

each restively harboring the same gift:

a fish

carved out of something cloud-
milkish,

neither soapstone and

not jade.

The all of them—

Sometimes holding the gift
out to us.

The gift throwing routinely up into sudden

relief

their invisible hands.

THE PINNACLE

Having found a trail, we
but followed. Technically,
you followed me. How

much is not what it looks like.
I'm remembering parts
so overgrown, I kept

stopping to ask which way
from here. You did not
ask this question. Each time

I looked back, you weren't
stopping, you were
following, you were not

asking questions. In time
we came to a sloped
meadow. The tall grass

made me nervous.
Though I explained,
I was not understood

entirely. You were patient,
you allowed me some
time to become

different. If I didn't
change, you didn't notice,
for I pushed forward,

crossing the meadow by
playing a game in my head
called *Cross the Meadow*

or Don't Cross It, by which
we arrived at the wooded
hemline of forest. The path

steepening upward, but
more clear. We ascended.
I am remembering

the obvious—trees
mostly, and a hardness of
breath that you said had

less to do with altitude
than with shape, our
being out of. To agree was

easy, and not binding. I
liked that. Almost like
pleasure, for a small

distance. I am including,
in particular, that sudden
denseness of ferns you

called a sea, and I said it
was like that—but
wasn't it also some over-

whelmingly green argument
whose point was that
not everything requires

light? You did not
answer, having not asked
that question. As when, if

frequently there were
sounds nothing visible
could account for, I did

not pursue them. What is
not related? I am still
remembering the feathers

—five of them, long, a
lightish brown with
darker brown stippling—

you found scattered to
one of the trail's sides. I
had missed them:

those of a turkey, as
you suggested—or, as
I said, a pheasant? When

you said I should
hold them, I thanked you.
I can appreciate small

gifts. I stopped thinking
what I was thinking—the
uncleanliness of birds—

and took them into
my hand. I arranged
the feathers into the rough

shape of a fan, and began,
like that, to feel cooler, more
sure: the pinnacle we'd been

told the trail led to would
come, the trail would end
in what they usually do,

a view. There are limited
choices. Already *Go
Down or Don't*, in my head.

FAMILIAR

Like the wrong dream
I shall very soon have
to live with (I can

tell that,
already),

or like some strong and
suddenly visible
possibility
toward a man who has known

better—

and I the man, and
without master—

the dog approaches.

He is running . . .

I am not
fearless, but have long
held—and knocked
wood to—a luck that

still comes—*May it
keep coming*, I'd said,

and now the dog: if

half leaping, then half,
too, falling

on me,
not the inevitably entire
weight of a man after,
in sleep,

but the partial weight that
a man instinctively gives

of himself,

during sex— less trust,
than doubt yielding
brief to a large,
to a want
increasing—

why does it seem, so much,
like that? A lost,

because—like
everything—losable,

a lost dog . . .

I take him into
that part of me
that has always taken the lost
in,

and his body
arches up into ache or
a statement:

If you understood me,
you would know

to help me:

Little one,

Sir,

will it matter?
If already I can tell how I

shall help him,
because I

do—I do understand him—?

CHOSEN FIGURE

"That was the winter of three
instances of
birds colliding
with the one window.

Each time—

superstition, or
else wisdom—I
asked, aloud,

Who has died?

        Each time, the glass
held, for answer."

*Like any man wanting
in instruction, he
did not say at first
the correct words,*

for he didn't know them.

Later though—
knowing them—that he did not
say the words
correctly:
          —That we found
unforgivable.

＠‾

Nothing, understand, to do with
you, who could be
any man now—now and wanting.

No questions. Not so much

Down-on-your-knees, as
Down-on-your-knees-*Sir*, had you

forgotten. A mirror likeness,
and what its glass holds, for answer.
A darkening spot upon

                    your brow,
where the Lord has touched you.

CARAVAN

Clarion,
boom-time,
yes—though, more often,

the almost-silence that the hum
of activity everywhere
now equals,

cliché, everywhere,
exaggeration,
lines like

It is as if I had known you
forever,
I had only to find you,

images like
water
and sand

and white birds
and—off of all of them—
the light shivering with

meaning, but one that
is difficult to
translate because

language should be—and
is—flexible,
it recalls, in

this way, morality,
how there's nothing, it
seems, not to be given

in to. Some
are swimming,
others scavenging

—coins,
          shells—
others struggle across

blankets whose
stones-as-anchors
routinely fail

at a new corner.
The corners at first
fluttering like truth, then

like the edges we
imagine for it.
I have been here before,

apparently. I am leading the way.

SAFARI FIGURE

An intention toward
damage—
or indifference—or merely

the languor that is reflection and having
too much of the world's
time to spend

on it: which of these
is the boy's face?
If a gatherer, then in

what capacity:
as any sportsman to, already, his
half-breathless

kill, shining?
or as one man helping
another step free of what

does not appear to
be, now that I look closely,
deep water?

First, I was a vessel,
holding one who had sought
enclosure.

Then the terms of need—
of themselves—reversed, only
incompletely:

he became as, for long,
I had been; and I—I was still
myself.

If this is my own hand at this—
my shirt, and
my collar—whose else

but mine, then,
the hand
loosening? whose, the hand that

binds fast? —If
a gentleman,
my face, or his, that I'm startled by?

YOURS, AND THE ROOM AFTER

I admit to entering them
both—no
force behind me

except my own—
but have since come
to believe I meant each time

nothing by it,
unless a kindness: granted,
a hard one. Prizing

clarity, I am rarely
without it, yet I have been
often not quite

understood—
The light
afforded by grand

windows, the as-if-
indecisively
thrown sheets, styled

tokens of dishevelment:
these become the facts
only insofar as they

misrepresent me. Can't
there always be found,
somewhere,

a sconced mirror in three
panels, say, to confirm
what is known

already: how many-sided is
the body, how inadequate
every mirror . . . ?

The rest, however—all of it—
sure, call true: did I
intend the single orchid,

do I intend
still its five flowers
open, its four

shut ones? Yes:
Water inside a bud vase the color
of water.

THE FIGURE, THE BOUNDARY, THE LIGHT

As he crosses the field, he is
easily all I mean by *the flesh
is small, is occasional*:

the grass he divides with
his body reuniting behind him
like too immediate a forgiveness;

even those birds that are least
remarkable do not notice, and
transcend him.

                    Questions like
*What is the difference between
intention and that space to which*

*any bird—merely and next—
comes?*
          To ask which, means

finally to resolve little, and lose
time. He has reached, almost,
the field's ending, which is trees:

birch, aspen; a third I cannot
call dissuasion, for he is entering,
has gone in.

                    Undeliberately,
on purpose.
                    As I have seen

before, a man touching what
he has not lost, but expects to.
The parts that are visible as,

already, the parts that are more
few. Like proof, omen, both,
just his hair, now—despite

shadow, still a brightness; its
dimming, that of anything—
chance,

          when it moves away.
As I understand it, I could
call him. Though it would help,

it is not required that I give him
a name first. Also, nothing
says he stops, then, or must turn.

REVISION

Which is worse—not being
myself, for long hours, able to

account for my own absence; or
not having been, by anyone,

asked to—I can't say. As when
the leaves have but to angle

in direct proportion to the wind's
force, times its direction,

and the mind, whose
instinct is to resist any

namelessness, calls
all of it—leaves, leaves,

and the wind's force—
trust, at first, then *disregard*

until, suspecting the truer name is
neither of these, it must

stop naming. Or as in
the days, reportedly, of

the gods having dwelled
among us—always

people invariably not knowing
and then (some irreducible

odor, an abrupt
solidity to the light) only then

knowing, but too late,
their faces changed

forever after by the difficult
weight of mere witness,

of having none but their own
word for it . . . If mistake, possibly,

yet mistake this
afternoon seems less

a river than a barely contained in
spite of everything

belief: there's another ending.
In this one, I recognize you—

and the recognizing has the effect of
slowing down that

part of me that would
walk past, or as if away toward

another ending—   You

speak first. And I'll answer.

ACKNOWLEDGMENTS

Grateful acknowledgment is made to the editors of the following journals, in which these poems first appeared:

Colorado Review: "The Figure, the Boundary, the Light," "Just South of the Kingdom," "Words of Love"

Field: "Tether"

Harvard Review: "Familiar"

The Iowa Review: "For the Falconer," "Lustrum," "Roman Glass"

The Kenyon Review: "Caravan," "The Pinnacle," "Recumbent," "Regalia Figure"

Literary Imagination: "Strung Absentia"

The Nation: "Luck," "Stagger"

New England Review: "Safari Figure"

The New Republic: "Preamble"

Provincetown Arts: "Little Dance Outside the Ruins of Unreason"

Slate: "The Point of the Lambs," "Spoils, Dividing"

TriQuarterly: "Chosen Figure," "The Lost Chorus," "Revision," "Yours, and the Room After"

"Chamber Music," "Little Dance Outside the Ruins of Unreason," "Recumbent," and "Regalia Figure" also appeared in *The Bread Loaf Anthology of New American Poets*, Michael Collier, ed., University Press of New England, 2000.

9 780374 528454